Original title:
One Heart, Whole

Copyright © 2024 Swan Charm
All rights reserved.

Author: Linda Leevike
ISBN HARDBACK: 978-9916-89-682-2
ISBN PAPERBACK: 978-9916-89-683-9
ISBN EBOOK: 978-9916-89-684-6

Within the Hands of Trusting Faith

In shadows deep, where hope may bend,
We seek the light that will not end.
With whispered prayers, our spirits rise,
Embracing love that never dies.

Each heartbeat echoes, pure and sweet,
In trust we walk, we will not cheat.
With open hearts, we share our plight,
And journey forth toward sacred light.

A Radiance of Togetherness

In the glow of evening's grace,
We gather here, in sacred space.
With hands entwined, our spirits soar,
Together found, forevermore.

Through trials faced and joys embraced,
In unity, our fears displaced.
Each voice a song, a harmony,
A testament to what can be.

Anchored in Sacred Bonds

In storms that rage, we stand as one,
With faith that shines, our battles won.
Each tethered heart, a sacred thread,
In love's embrace, no fear or dread.

The anchor holds, through tempest's might,
In every tear, we find the light.
With courage bold, we lift each other,
In every friend, we see a brother.

The Sacred River of Unity

Flowing gently, love's embrace,
A river wide, a sacred space.
In every journey, hand in hand,
Together carved, we make our stand.

From mountains high to valleys low,
The sacred stream of kindness flows.
With open hearts, our dreams entwined,
In unity, true peace we find.

Together in Sacred Promise

In the garden of our hearts, we bow,
United in purpose, sacred vow.
Hand in hand, we walk this way,
Seeking light in every day.

With whispers soft, our spirits soar,
In every trial, we seek for more.
Faith like a river, flowing free,
Together, we find our peace in thee.

Echoes of Faith Intertwined

In the quiet night, a prayer ascends,
Echoing softly, where love transcends.
Voices mingle, a chorus divine,
In harmony, our hearts align.

With every step, we tread as one,
In the warmth of the morning sun.
Faith woven deep, like threads of gold,
In our unity, the truth unfolds.

In the Sanctuary of Togetherness

Within these walls, our spirits blend,
A sacred space where hearts commend.
With every word, we bless our days,
In love's embrace, we find our ways.

Together we rise, in prayer we stand,
Bound by trust, united hand in hand.
In the sanctuary of our grace,
We discover joy in each face.

Threads of Light

In the tapestry of life, we weave,
Threads of light, in love we believe.
Each stitch a promise, each knot a chance,
Together we flourish, in faith we dance.

From darkness into dawn, we find our path,
Guided by love, we escape the wrath.
With hearts ablaze, our spirits soar,
Threads of light connect us more.

Woven Together

In the loom of grace, our lives entwine,
Crafted by hands that are divine.
Every heartbeat, a song we sing,
Woven together, our offerings bring.

Through trials faced and mountains climbed,
In unity, our souls aligned.
With every prayer and whisper shared,
In love's embrace, we are prepared.

Eternal Embrace

In the quiet glow of holy light,
Hearts entwined in sacred flight.
Bound by faith, we journey on,
In grace we find where hope is drawn.

Through trials faced, our spirits soar,
In every breath, we seek the more.
Together we rise, hand in hand,
In love's embrace, we make our stand.

The Sanctity of Unity

A melody of voices blend,
In harmony, our souls transcend.
Each difference a thread we weave,
In love's embrace, we all believe.

From mountains high to valleys low,
In every heart, compassion grows.
We gather strength from diverse views,
In unity, we softly choose.

A Tapestry of Souls

Each thread a tale of joy and pain,
Together we are bound, not in vain.
Colors bright, yet shadows cast,
In every stitch, our prayers are vast.

With every heartbeat, stories merge,
In sacred dance, we all converge.
A tapestry of hopes and dreams,
In every whisper, love redeems.

Whispers of the Divine Connection

In the stillness, we hear the call,
A gentle voice that echoes all.
In moments pure, divinely blessed,
We find our peace, within our quest.

Through every trial, a lesson shared,
Faith ignites, for love has spared.
In quiet times, we seek the light,
In whispers soft, we find our might.

Merging of Minds

In the stillness, thoughts arise,
Unity found, beneath vast skies.
Wisdom shared, a sacred link,
Where hearts and souls begin to think.

Echoes whisper from afar,
Guiding light, a shining star.
Bridges forged in purest trust,
In love's embrace, we rise from dust.

Joining of Hearts

Two hearts beating, a sacred bond,
In realms of grace, beyond the dawn.
With every prayer, we intertwine,
A tapestry of love divine.

Voices lift in joyous song,
In harmony, where we belong.
With open hands, we share the light,
Guiding each other through the night.

Celestial Flames: A Dance of Spirits

In the heavens, fires ignite,
Dancing spirits, pure delight.
With every flame, a story told,
Of love's embrace, and hearts of gold.

Through the ether, they entwine,
A cosmic waltz, so divine.
In eternal rhythm, they sway,
Igniting dreams in night's ballet.

Lifted by Communion

In sacred circles, we unite,
Hearts raised high, embracing light.
With every word, a prayer ascends,
In unity, where love transcends.

Together we stand, side by side,
In faith's embrace, we shall abide.
With every breath, we find our way,
In the warmth of love's array.

Breath of the Infinite

In the stillness, we inhale grace,
A moment's pause, a sacred space.
With every breath, the spirit grows,
Awakening love, as river flows.

Infinite whispers fill the air,
Guidance offered, in heartfelt prayer.
Together we journey, hand in hand,
With faith as our guide, we understand.

From Many, One Light

In the dawn of creation's grace,
Many paths converge in space.
Gathered hearts, a single call,
In the shadow of the All.

Waves of faith in unity,
Bound by threads of humble plea.
Shining bright, through storm and strife,
One true Light, the gift of Life.

In the silence, whispers speak,
Finding strength in what is weak.
Together we rise, hand in hand,
For in love, we firmly stand.

From valleys low to mountains high,
Echos of a sweetened sigh.
In our voices, a gentle tune,
We are one beneath the moon.

As we journey, hearts ignite,
Drawing warmth from One True Light.
From many souls, a perfect blend,
In love's embrace, we shall transcend.

In the Realm of Love's Unity

In the realm where hearts unite,
Love's embrace dispels the night.
Boundless joy in every glance,
In harmony, we find our dance.

Every tear, a lesson learned,
Each flame of hope, brightly burned.
Together, we weave the thread,
In love's garden, all is fed.

Through trials faced, we grow wise,
Finding grace in each sunrise.
In every hug, a story shared,
A testament of love declared.

In every voice, a sacred song,
In unity, we all belong.
Though diverse, our spirits soar,
In love's unity, forevermore.

Let us gather, hand in hand,
In this holy, promised land.
For in love's light, we ignite,
In the realm of purest sight.

Beneath the Stars of Togetherness

Beneath the stars, our hopes align,
In the quiet, hearts combine.
Hand in hand, through darkest night,
We find solace in the light.

Every twinkle tells a tale,
Of love that never will grow stale.
A grand design, in every heart,
From the whole, we never part.

In the whispers of the breeze,
Our shared dreams float with such ease.
As the moon casts shadows deep,
In togetherness, we shall keep.

Each moment shared, a sacred bliss,
In unity, we find our kiss.
Though the world may churn and sway,
Together, we shall find our way.

In the vastness, one we stand,
A gentle, loving, guiding hand.
Beneath the stars, love shines bright,
In togetherness, we find our light.

The Covenant of Together

In the promise of the dawn,
We gather, every fear withdrawn.
In the circle, spirits blend,
The covenant of love transcends.

Every heartbeat, softly beats,
In unity, the heart repeats.
From the ashes, we arise,
In our bond, the sacred ties.

Through the storms, we sail as one,
With every battle fought and won.
In laughter shared and tears we weep,
We forge a vow, steadfast and deep.

In the garden where love grows,
Through every season, it bestows.
A tapestry of light and grace,
In this covenant, we embrace.

Bound by faith, we walk this road,
In every step, love's heavy load.
Together, let our anthem swell,
In the covenant, all is well.

Hearts Bound in Sacred Vows

In whispers soft, we pledge our hearts,
With sacred vows that never part.
Through trials faced, our spirits soar,
Together bound, forevermore.

With every breath, we seek the light,
In faith and love, we find our might.
Through storms and shadows, hand in hand,
In unity, together we stand.

The holy bond, a radiant thread,
In love's embrace, the tears we shed.
A tapestry of grace we weave,
In every promise, we believe.

Through faith renewed, our souls ignite,
In every dawn, a future bright.
Together blessed, forever true,
In every vow, a world anew.

In sacred space, where love expands,
Two hearts as one, our journey strands.
With spirits fused, we rise and shine,
In sacred vows, forever thine.

Beneath the Wings of Divine Concord

In shadows cast, we find our grace,
Beneath His wings, a warm embrace.
In gentle whispers, prayers align,
In harmony, our hearts entwine.

The trials faced, like storms that blow,
Within the light, our spirits flow.
With hands uplifted, voices blend,
In love's sweet song, our hearts defend.

In every heartbeat, echoes soar,
United souls, forevermore.
Through every sorrow, joy revealed,
In sacred balance, hearts are healed.

With every dawn, a promise new,
In faith we walk, both strong and true.
Beneath the wings, we seek the way,
In love's embrace, we choose to stay.

As stars align in velvet skies,
In every tear, a love that ties.
With open hearts, we take our flight,
Beneath divine, our paths alight.

The Celestial Quilt of Souls

A tapestry of love so bright,
Woven stars in the velvet night.
In every thread, a story spun,
A quilt of souls, forever one.

In warmth we wrap, in unity,
Through every joy, our spirits free.
In moments shared, a glance, a touch,
Each heartbeat sings, our love is such.

With every patch, a tale retold,
In sacred bonds, we find our gold.
Beneath the seams, the whispers thrive,
In dreams we share, we come alive.

Through trials faced and paths unknown,
In faith we stand, we've brightly grown.
With open hearts, we greet the morn,
In love's embrace, the new is born.

The stars above, they guide our way,
In every night, we find the day.
A celestial quilt, our spirits glow,
Together held, in love we flow.

In the Arms of Shared Grace

In tender moments, grace unfolds,
Within our hearts, the warmth it holds.
In every tear, a tale we share,
In love's embrace, we breathe the air.

Through valleys low and peaks so high,
In each other's arms, our spirits fly.
With gentle hands, we lift the bowed,
In faith, we stand, forever proud.

The light of dawn, a beacon bright,
In unity, we find our flight.
With whispered prayers, our souls align,
In shared grace, your hand in mine.

Through shadows cast, we shine anew,
With every step, a pledge so true.
In every heartbeat, love conveys,
In the arms of shared grace, we raise.

In sacred time, our spirits blend,
With every blessing, hearts transcend.
To walk this path, a gift bestowed,
In love's embrace, our spirits flowed.

The Symphony of Shared Faith

In the stillness of the night,
Voices rise, a gentle choir,
Echoes of a love divine,
Binding hearts in sacred fire.

Together we walk His path,
Hand in hand through trials faced,
Finding solace in our trust,
In His mercy, we are graced.

Every prayer a whispered song,
Melodies of hope and grace,
In the heart of community,
We find our sacred space.

As we gather, spirits soar,
Each soul a note in the hymn,
A symphony of shared faith,
In His light, we will not dim.

For in unity, we are strong,
With love as our guiding star,
Together, we journey forth,
Knowing He is never far.

Reflections of a Sacred Bond

In quiet moments, let us see,
Reflections of His grace abound,
Mirrored in each other's eyes,
In love's embrace, we are found.

With every whispered prayer at dawn,
We nurture the sacred tie,
A bond that time cannot sever,
As the heavens paint the sky.

Through trials and through joy we share,
Each tear and laughter intertwined,
In His light, we find our way,
A love that's true and divinely kind.

Together we rise in faith,
Voices entwined, strong and clear,
Navigating life's vast sea,
Our souls anchored, free from fear.

For in every heartbeat echoes,
The whispers of a love profound,
A sacred bond, unbreakable,
In His grace, we are forever bound.

Unity in the Eyes of Creation

From the mountains to the seas,
Creation sings a perfect tune,
In the whisper of the breeze,
A melody of love attuned.

Each flower blooms, a testament,
In colors bright, pure and true,
A tapestry of life divine,
Woven with a sacred view.

In the eyes of every creature,
We find a spark of the divine,
Unity in life's embrace,
A love that transcends all time.

Together, we lift our voices,
In harmony, we stand as one,
For in His creation's beauty,
The story of love is spun.

Through the stars that light the night,
To the dawn's first gentle ray,
In unity, we celebrate,
The gift of life, come what may.

The Light Within Us All

In the darkness, a flame flickers,
A light within, pure and bright,
Guiding us through the shadows,
A beacon of hope, our insight.

Every soul, a spark divine,
Illuminating the path ahead,
In this dance of life we share,
With love, we are gently led.

When the world feels overwhelming,
And the night seems long and cold,
Remember the light within us,
A warmth that can never be sold.

For together, we shine brighter,
In unity, our hearts align,
A constellation of spirits,
In His love, across space, they twine.

So let your light shine boldly,
In every moment, be the call,
For we are reflections of Him,
The light within us, in us all.

Hearts Entwined in Faith's Embrace

In quiet prayer, our spirits rise,
Lifted high beneath holy skies.
Bound together, our hearts align,
In faith's embrace, our souls combine.

Through trials faced, we stand as one,
Guided bright by the setting sun.
With every tear, our strength renews,
In love's pure light, we share our views.

The path is steep, yet we walk near,
In whispered hope, we shed our fear.
Together, striving toward the light,
Faith's embrace, our endless might.

In sacred bonds, we find our way,
Hearts entwined, come what may.
With open arms, we greet the dawn,
In unity, we journey on.

The Fabric of Unity Woven with Care

Threads of kindness stitch our hearts,
Together woven, never apart.
In every act, a subtle grace,
A tapestry time can't erase.

With hands extended, we build and grow,
In every smile, our love will show.
A fabric made of trust and peace,
In unity's song, our worries cease.

Each color bright, a story told,
In every heart, a warmth to hold.
Together we stand, diverse yet one,
In faith's pure light, we shine like the sun.

Embracing differences, we find our strength,
In spirit's journey, we go the length.
A world enriched, our spirits soar,
Woven with care, forevermore.

In the Light of Divine Kinship

In every prayer, a connection thrives,
In shared belief, our spirit drives.
With open hearts, we seek the truth,
In love's embrace, we find our youth.

Each moment shared, a gift we give,
Together we learn, together we live.
In sacred trust, our futures blend,
In divine kinship, we transcend.

With every blessing, we grow as one,
In light's embrace, our fears are undone.
Through trials faced and joys divine,
In faith's sweet bond, our souls entwine.

In harmony, we sing the song,
Of kinship strong, where all belong.
In every whisper, in every sigh,
We rise together, reaching high.

Reflections of Grace in Quiet Love

In stillness found, grace takes its flight,
In quiet love, we seek the light.
Reflections shine in gentle ways,
In every heart, a spirit plays.

The warmth of kindness softly flows,
In every seed of hope that grows.
With open arms, we shelter hearts,
In love's embrace, true peace imparts.

Through darkest nights, a star will gleam,
In moments shared, we dare to dream.
Together bound, with faith we stand,
In quiet love, we join hands.

With whispers tender, we cultivate,
A garden bright to celebrate.
In every tear, in every smile,
Reflections of grace stretch mile by mile.

The Still Waters of Collective Joy

In tranquil streams, our spirits meet,
Where love flows gently, pure and sweet.
In harmony, we lift our voice,
Together in faith, we rejoice.

With hearts united, we embrace,
A sacred bond, transcending space.
In stillness, grace awakens here,
As joy radiates, crystal clear.

Each drop reflects a vibrant hue,
A testament to what is true.
In every smile, in every tear,
The still waters draw us near.

In gratitude, we share this peace,
A love that longs, a sweet release.
With every whisper, every song,
We find the path where we belong.

So let us gather, hand in hand,
In this divine, enchanted land.
For in our hearts, a light will grow,
In still waters, collective joy flows.

The Dance of Interfaith Hearts

In twilight's glow, we lift our gaze,
A dance unfolds in sacred ways.
Each rhythm beats, a prayer in flight,
Hearts entwined, we seek the light.

From every corner, voices rise,
In unity, our spirits fly.
With grace and love, we intertwine,
As interfaith hearts begin to shine.

Together, we celebrate the flame,
In vibrant colors, we proclaim.
A tapestry of faith and hope,
In this grand dance, we learn to cope.

In every step, a story told,
A sacred truth, a heart of gold.
As we embrace the diverse spark,
Our souls ignite, igniting dark.

So let us move with joy and grace,
In this communion, we find our place.
For in the dance, we hear the call,
Interfaith hearts, united, we stand tall.

Where the Heartbeat of the Universe Resounds

In silence deep, we hear the beat,
A cosmic pulse, both pure and sweet.
With every breath, we sense the flow,
Where stars and whispers gently glow.

In every heartbeat, life reveals,
The sacred truths that love conceals.
Together, we seek the eternal flame,
In the universe, we call each name.

Through darkened skies, we find the way,
With faith as lantern, night turns to day.
In harmony with all we see,
The universe beats, alive and free.

As dawn arrives, we raise a prayer,
For every soul, in love, we care.
With open hearts and arms so wide,
We gather all, in peace abide.

In the heartbeat's echo, we belong,
A symphony, a sacred song.
For in this rhythm, we are found,
Where the heartbeat of the universe resounds.

The Spirit's Melody Unfolding Together

In quiet moments, the spirit sings,
A melody of peace it brings.
With every note, hearts intertwine,
In sacred unity, love will shine.

Together, we embrace each chord,
In harmony, we lift the word.
With hands joined tight, we build the song,
In spirit's melody, we belong.

Through trials faced and shadows cast,
A symphony that ever lasts.
In every struggle, joy will sway,
As we unfold, come what may.

The notes of love will guide our way,
In every heart, a bright bouquet.
Together, we shall weave the sound,
In spirit's melody, we are found.

So let us ever walk as one,
With every song, we have begun.
For in this harmony, we find,
The spirit's melody, intertwined.

Kindred Spirits in Divine Harmony

In the light of grace we stand,
Voices raised in whispered prayer.
Hearts entwined, hand in hand,
In each soul, Your love we share.

Winds of peace around us blow,
Guiding paths we cannot see.
In Your wisdom, we shall grow,
To one another, always free.

Mountains high and valleys low,
Reflect the joy of life we find.
United in this sacred flow,
God's embrace, our hearts aligned.

When darkness falls, we light the flame,
In every trial, spirits rise.
In His name, we speak the same,
Each challenge, a gift in disguise.

Together we will journey forth,
Through storms and calms, we stay the course.
In our bond, we find our worth,
A living testament, His source.

The Circle of Life's Blessing

In the dawn of morning's light,
Creation sings a pure refrain.
Each heartbeat echoes sacred night,
Life's brief journey, sweet and plain.

Underneath the starry skies,
We gather threads of hope and grace.
In every tear, a love that ties,
Connecting us in time and space.

Seasons shift and blossoms bloom,
Nature's cycle, strong and vast.
In every ending, new life's loom,
Promise whispers of the past.

With open hearts, we share the song,
An anthem of the earth and sky.
In fellowship, we all belong,
Together, we shall rise and fly.

In the circle, hand in hand,
Treading paths made bright by faith.
Each soul a note, a wondrous band,
In this life, we find our wraith.

In the Weave of Divine Love

Threads of mercy intertwined,
In the tapestry of grace.
Each stitch a purpose clearly signed,
Crafted with love, we find our place.

From every heart, a story spun,
In the loom of sacred trust.
Life's design reveals the One,
In bright colors, hope's adjust.

Through valleys deep, and mountains high,
Your presence is our guiding thread.
In Your arms, we will not die,
For in Your love, we are fed.

When shadows fall and doubts arise,
We turn to You, our strength, our light.
In every tear, the promise lies,
We journey forward, through the night.

In the weave of life, we find,
The beauty of each soul combined.
United hearts are consonant,
In Your love, our spirits blind.

Sacred Resonance

In the stillness, whispers call,
Echoes of a timeless grace.
Harmony in every fall,
Finding solace in Your face.

Every heartbeat, pulsing prayer,
Resonating through the night.
In Your love, we learn to care,
Guided by Your holy light.

Mountains echo with our song,
Songs that tremble through the air.
In Your presence, we belong,
Hearts aligned in love we share.

Waves of mercy wash the shore,
In the tides of hope, we rise.
Each note we sing, an open door,
In Your spirit, our hearts fly.

In this sacred resonance,
Together, we shall take our stand.
A symphony of love immense,
With You, O Lord, we understand.

The Unbreakable Thread

In shadows cast by doubt and fear,
A thread of hope is always near.
It weaves through hearts, a silent bond,
A guiding light, forever fond.

With every tear, a prayer ascends,
In unity, our spirit mends.
The fabric of our souls entwined,
A testament to love defined.

Through trials faced and mountains climbed,
This thread remains, forever primed.
A tapestry of faith so bright,
In darkness, shines with steadfast light.

When strife assails and tempests roar,
The thread pulls tight, endures and soars.
Each stitch a promise, strong and true,
Together, we'll see this journey through.

So clasp this thread with hands held tight,
For in its weave, we find our might.
United in spirit, hearts aflame,
In love's embrace, we rise, proclaim.

Illuminated by Faith's River

In tranquil waters, faith flows deep,
A current strong, our souls to keep.
Through valleys low and mountains steep,
In God's embrace, we find our leap.

Each ripple sings of grace and peace,
A melody that will not cease.
Though storms may come, we will not fear,
For in this river, Love is near.

Reflecting light through every trial,
Faith's river carries on in style.
Its path is lit by hope's embrace,
Guiding us to a sacred place.

With every step upon this shore,
We taste a truth we can't ignore.
Together flowing, hand in hand,
In faith's river, we make our stand.

A journey blessed, a trust so pure,
In faith's embrace, we will endure.
Each heart, a vessel, journeys free,
Illuminated by love's decree.

The Tides of Divine Togetherness

In every wave, a whisper calls,
The sea of faith where love enthralls.
Together we rise, together we fall,
In divine tides, we answer the call.

The moonlight dances on reflection,
Guiding hearts with gentle direction.
As tides of trust weave us as one,
We journey forth, our race begun.

Through ebb and flow, we understand,
In every crest, a sacred hand.
With spirits merged, we cleanse our fears,
In harmony, we shed our tears.

The ocean vast, its depths profound,
In unity, our faith unbound.
These tides bring solace, calm and grace,
Together we find our sacred place.

As we share in every tide,
In love's embrace, we will abide.
The rhythm of hearts, a symphony,
In divine togetherness, we are free.

The Harmony Within

In silence deep, a sacred sound,
A harmony that knows no bound.
Within each heart, a tune resides,
A song of hope where love abides.

Through trials faced, the melody grows,
In every tear, a beauty shows.
Each note, a prayer, a whispered plea,
In unity, we long to be free.

By candlelight, our spirits twine,
The harmony together, divine.
In every chord, a whisper of grace,
Resonating in time and space.

With open hearts, we share this song,
In love's embrace, we all belong.
The rhythm of life, in sync, we find,
A sacred bond that frees the mind.

So let us raise our voices clear,
In harmony, we conquer fear.
Together singing, hearts entwine,
In sacred space, our souls align.

Sacred Bonds Beneath the Stars

In the night sky, divine light shines,
Guiding our hearts, binding our minds.
With each whisper, a prayer takes flight,
We find our strength in the sacred night.

Beneath the heavens, our spirits rise,
In unity forged, we seek the prize.
Hand in hand, through shadows we tread,
With faith as our compass, love as our thread.

Each star a beacon, each wish a plea,
For peace and light, in harmony.
Together we journey, through trials and grace,
Our souls entwined in this sacred space.

In the silence, a promise is heard,
Echoed in hearts, unspoken word.
For in this bond, our spirits lay bare,
Together we stand, in the warmth of prayer.

So let us gather, beneath this expanse,
In reverence we share, in love we dance.
A tapestry woven, by hands that create,
The sacred bonds that shall never abate.

The Essence of Togetherness

In the dawn's light, we rise as one,
Two souls united, a journey begun.
With hearts open wide, we embrace the day,
In the essence of love, we find our way.

Through trials faced, we stand side by side,
In laughter and tears, our spirits reside.
Each moment a treasure, each breath a song,
In the essence of togetherness, we belong.

With every heartbeat, a rhythm divine,
A dance of connection, your hand in mine.
In gathering strength, our light shall shine,
In this essence of unity, our hearts entwine.

Through valleys low and mountains steep,
In the sanctity of trust, our promises keep.
The essence of life, a flow that sustains,
Binds us together, through joys and pains.

So let us cherish this gift we share,
In every glance, in every prayer.
For in togetherness, our spirits soar,
In the essence of love, forevermore.

Celestial Threads of Connection

In the night sky, threads of gold,
Woven by hands, both gentle and bold.
Each star a story, each light a guide,
In celestial bonds, together we'll bide.

We gather under the vastness above,
Spun from the fabric of faith and love.
In the silent whispers of the twilight breeze,
Our hearts unite, as the world finds peace.

Each dawn a promise, each dusk a prayer,
In the tapestry of life, we lay our care.
With threads unseen, yet vibrant and strong,
We journey together, where souls belong.

Through storms that rage and calm that follows,
In each other's strength, our spirit swallows.
With celestial threads, we weave our fate,
Bound by connection, it's never too late.

So look to the stars, let your heart believe,
In the bonds of connection, we find what we weave.
For life is a canvas, and love is the art,
In celestial threads, we shall never part.

In the Garden of Shared Grace

In a garden where flowers bloom bright,
We cultivate love with grace and light.
Each petal a promise, each stem a sign,
In the garden of grace, your hand in mine.

With hearts like seeds, we plant our dreams,
Watered with kindness, nourished by beams.
In this sacred soil, our spirits embrace,
In the garden of grace, we find our place.

With whispers of faith and laughter's sweet sound,
In the tapestry of life, deep roots are found.
Together we flourish, with care we tend,
In the garden of grace, love knows no end.

Through seasons we journey, hand in hand,
In the beauty of sharing, together we'll stand.
For every bloom tells a story of trust,
In the garden of grace, it's love that's a must.

So let us rejoice, for this is our fate,
In the garden of grace, love shall create.
With every heartbeat, and each soft embrace,
We blossom together, in divine space.

The Celestial Circle of Belief

In twilight's glow, our spirits soar,
Each whispered prayer, a sacred lore.
The stars above, a guiding light,
We gather close, in love's pure sight.

The circle formed, both strong and true,
In silence shared, our hearts renew.
With open arms, we seek the divine,
Embracing faith, our souls entwine.

Through trials faced, we stand as one,
For in this bond, no work is done.
Each tear we shed, a strength in grace,
Reflecting love, in every space.

The echoes of the past resound,
In every heart, a home is found.
We lift our voices, a chorus strong,
In unity, we all belong.

As time unfolds, the journey flows,
In fields of faith, a garden grows.
With every step, we find our way,
In celestial light, we trust and stay.

When Hearts Converge in Prayer

In twilight's calm, our voices rise,
To meet the heavens, to touch the skies.
With humble hearts, we seek your grace,
In sacred space, we find our place.

The silence wraps us in its care,
Our burdens lifted, a shared prayer.
In faith we stand, with lifted hands,
United strong, wherever we land.

Each heartbeat echoes, love's sweet call,
In every tear, we rise and fall.
The bonds we share, a sacred thread,
In prayer's embrace, our fears are shed.

The light within, a guiding star,
In shared intent, we wander far.
With gentle words and steadfast sighs,
We weave our hopes, as time flies by.

When hearts align, a miracle,
In love's own dance, we feel the pull.
Together in spirit, hand in hand,
In love and prayer, we always stand.

The Sacred Union of Common Dreams

In shadowed light, our visions blend,
Stitching the seams of hope we send.
With open minds, we seek the same,
A tapestry of love, not fame.

The dreams we share ignite the night,
In quiet whispers, they take flight.
Harmonious hearts beat as one,
Guided by stars, our journey's begun.

Together we rise, through trials we face,
In every heartbeat, we find our place.
Our sacred union, a blessed bond,
In shared dreams, we grow beyond.

With courage bold, we chase the dawn,
In hope renewed, our doubts are gone.
For in this dream, together we're strong,
In laughter and light, where we belong.

Each soul a note in love's great song,
In harmony, we know we belong.
Together we weave our future bright,
In sacred dreams, we take our flight.

Joining Hands in Quiet Devotion

In stillness found, our hands unite,
With every clasp, a promise bright.
Through trials faced, together we stand,
In quiet devotion, hand in hand.

The time we share, a sacred gift,
In moments cherished, our spirits lift.
With gentle hearts and souls laid bare,
We find our strength in humble prayer.

In every heartbeat, we hear a song,
A melody where all belong.
As whispers fade, we listen deep,
In quietude, our dreams we keep.

Through paths unknown, our faith will guide,
In love's embrace, we shall abide.
For every hand that seeks to hold,
Is a tale of love, forever told.

In sacred space, our spirits blend,
In joining hands, we find the end.
Together moving, a journey shared,
In quiet devotion, forever paired.

When Spirits Meet in Prayerful Stillness

In quiet nights, we gather near,
To share our whispers, pure and clear.
The sacred bond, so strong, we weave,
In stillness found, we truly believe.

Heaven's grace descends like dew,
With every heart, a sacred view.
In silence, souls begin to dance,
A holy moment, a blessed chance.

Voices blend in softest hymn,
As shadows fade and lights grow dim.
Through reverence, we stand as one,
In prayerful stillness, all is done.

The spirit flows like gentle streams,
United in our waking dreams.
With every breath, we praise the peace,
In stillness, hearts begin to cease.

Together here, we find the grace,
In every tear, we find our place.
When spirits meet, the love ignites,
In prayerful stillness, pure delights.

The Meeting of Hearts in Sacred Space

In sacred spaces, hearts align,
With whispers soft, their love entwined.
Each open heart, a gentle flame,
In unity, we share one name.

Beneath the grace of heaven's light,
We gather close throughout the night.
In timeless bonds, our souls connect,
In sacred space, we find respect.

Hands uplifted, spirits soar,
In love and prayer, we seek for more.
Where dreams converge and hopes arise,
Our meeting place, the endless skies.

With every heartbeat, faith renews,
In silent strength, the spirit brews.
Together, we embrace the call,
In sacred space, love conquers all.

So let us gather, while we can,
In timeless moments, hand in hand.
The meeting of hearts brings us grace,
In sacred space, a warm embrace.

The Eternal Bond Across Time

Through ages past, our spirits roam,
In rivers deep, they find a home.
No distance great, nor time that binds,
The sacred strands, our heart entwined.

With every breath, our echoes blend,
In a dance of souls that never end.
The ties we share, a radiant thread,
In eternal love, where fears are shed.

Each moment spent, a cherished gift,
As time unravels, spirits lift.
The stories weave through starry skies,
With every glance, the bond replies.

From past to present, we remain,
In whispered prayers, love's refrain.
A timeless bond, forever near,
In every heartbeat, we are here.

So let us honor what's intertwined,
In every truth, a love defined.
Across the years, our spirits dance,
The eternal bond, a sacred chance.

Where Light Meets Love's True Essence

In gardens bright, where sunlight plays,
Love's essence blooms through all our days.
With every ray, a heart ignites,
In joyful moments, love invites.

As shadows fall and twilight grows,
The light reveals what kindness shows.
In every smile, the warmth we find,
Where love meets light, we leave behind.

In gentle waves and breezes sweet,
Our souls entwine, in harmony meet.
With every touch, the spirit bends,
Where light converges, love transcends.

In stillness found, a sacred shift,
A glowing gift, the spirit's lift.
In depth of night, we see the way,
Where light meets love, we freely pray.

Together here, we stand as one,
In light and love, the battles won.
With open hearts, forever blessed,
Where light meets love, we find our rest.

A Covenant of Souls in Reverence

In the stillness of the night, we pray,
His whispers grace our solemn way.
Beneath the stars that brightly shine,
We gather in love, hearts entwined.

Bound by faith, our spirits rise,
With every breath, our souls harmonize.
In unity, we seek the light,
Together, we embrace the night.

O gentle hands that guide our course,
We find our strength in sacred force.
Through trials faced and burdens borne,
In His love, we are reborn.

The promises we hold so dear,
In echoing prayers, we draw near.
Each heart a vessel, pure and true,
A covenant forged in endless view.

May our voices rise in sweet refrain,
In love's embrace, we break all chains.
For in this bond, we find our home,
A sacred journey, never alone.

The Dance of Divine Interlink

In the harmony of grace, we sway,
Each step a prayer, soft as the day.
With every heartbeat, heaven's song,
Entwined as one, where we belong.

The rhythm flows through veins of light,
Guided by spirits, pure and bright.
In circles drawn by fate's sweet hand,
Together we rise, together we stand.

With whispers of love that fill the air,
We dance on paths of endless care.
In joyous union, we sing and twirl,
Our souls alight in a sacred whirl.

Each note a blessing, a gift divine,
In every glance, His love we find.
With faith as our partner, bold and true,
In this dance, forever we renew.

As the stars guide our sacred flight,
We celebrate this holy night.
For in our dance, we're not just one,
In unity, our journey's begun.

Hearts Alight in Holy Union

In the soft glow of dawn's embrace,
Hearts awaken, filled with grace.
Beneath the sky, a sacred choir,
We lift our souls, lifted higher.

In every prayer, a promise sealed,
A love in light, forever revealed.
With gentle hands, He binds our fate,
In holy union, we celebrate.

Each moment shared, a treasured gift,
In unity, our spirits lift.
In silence, we hear the calling clear,
A bond of love that draws us near.

Through trials faced, we stand as one,
In faith and trust, our battles won.
With hearts alight, we shine so bright,
A beacon true in darkest night.

For love is found in every tear,
In moments cherished, hearts sincere.
Together we walk this sacred land,
In holy union, hand in hand.

The Bridge of Spirit's Kinship

On the river of life, we build a bridge,
With faith's strong arms, we cross each ridge.
In harmony, our spirits blend,
Connected paths that never end.

With whispers of love, the water flows,
In every heart, the truth bestows.
With every step, spiritual grace,
United in our sacred space.

Through valleys low and mountains high,
Together we reach for the sky.
In every sunset, every dawn,
A kinship forged, forever strong.

As we traverse this sacred bridge,
In trust and hope, we break each ridge.
With every heartbeat, a promise made,
In Spirit's love, we'll never fade.

For in this journey, we find our role,
In every story, a shared soul.
Together as one, we choose to be,
The bridge of kinship, wild and free.

The Light of Faith

In shadows deep, the light appears,
A beacon bright, to calm our fears.
Through trials faced, we find our way,
With faith as guide, we choose to stay.

In whispered prayers, our hopes ascend,
For every heart, a truth to mend.
With open arms, the spirit flows,
In love we trust, the faith still grows.

Each step we take, the path unrolled,
In every heart, a story told.
The dawn shall break, our joys ignite,
For in our souls, we find the light.

Together strong, we walk this quest,
In unity, we find our rest.
Through valleys low, and mountains high,
With faith in hand, we reach the sky.

So let us shine, with hearts ablaze,
In every moment, sing His praise.
The light of faith, our guiding star,
Will lead us home, no matter how far.

Reflected Brightly

In mirrors bright, His love reflects,
A tapestry of sweet connects.
For every soul, a sacred bond,
In faith we rise, and love responds.

When darkness falls, the light remains,
With gentle whispers, hope sustains.
Through trials fierce, we stand as one,
Reflecting light, till day is done.

In every smile, a glimpse divine,
In hands held tight, our hearts entwine.
The beauty found in shared embrace,
A kindred spirit, sacred space.

Let love be felt, in every tear,
For through the pain, our path is clear.
In unity, our purpose shines,
In every heart, His love aligns.

So let us walk, with grace and light,
Reflected brightly, through day and night.
In every breath, His presence near,
Together strong, we have no fear.

A Covenant of Love in Togetherness

In unity, we find our creed,
A covenant strong, in every deed.
With hearts in sync, and spirits free,
In love we flourish, in harmony.

Through trials met, and joys we share,
In sacred trust, we show we care.
Each voice a song, in sweet array,
Together bound, we'll find our way.

With open hearts, and hands entwined,
In every moment, love aligned.
Through storms we weather, side by side,
In faith we stand, our hearts our guide.

Let kindness flow, in every glance,
In every step, a holy dance.
A tapestry of light we weave,
In love's embrace, we all believe.

So let us cherish, this sacred bond,
In togetherness, our souls respond.
A covenant forged, in trust and grace,
In love we find, our sacred place.

When Souls Sing in Resonance

In sacred space, our voices soar,
When souls unite, we reach for more.
With harmony, our hearts align,
In melodies, the love divine.

Each note we sing, a prayer released,\nIn joy we gather,
our hearts increased.
For every song, a story told,
In resonant love, we break the mold.

When trials come, we'll still rejoice,
Together strong, we'll raise our voice.
In every tear, a lesson learned,
In faith we trust, and hearts are burned.

Through valleys low, and mountains grand,
In rhythm found, we take a stand.
With open hearts, the song we write,
In sacred truth, we find the light.

So let us gather, in joy's embrace,
In every note, we find our grace.
When souls sing out, in purest form,
In resonance, our spirits warm.

The Sacred Gathering of Hearts

In sacred gathering, hearts entwine,
Together we share, a love divine.
With every breath, a prayer we'll weave,
In this embrace, we do believe.

As spirits lifted, hopes take flight,
In unity, we seek the light.
Our voices blend, a sweet refrain,
In love's embrace, we break the chain.

Through laughter shared, and tears that flow,
In sacred trust, our spirits grow.
With open arms, we welcome all,
In every heart, we heed the call.

Let kindness reign, in every glance,
Together we rise, in faith's expanse.
In this gathering, our souls align,
In love's embrace, we feel divine.

So let us stand, hand in hand, we vow,
In this sacred moment, here and now.
The gathering of hearts, a timeless art,
In every soul, we find our part.

United in Spirit's Embrace

In the light of grace we stand,
Hand in hand, across the land,
Hearts entwined in sacred song,
Together in the love so strong.

Beneath the stars, we seek the way,
In every night, a hopeful day,
Voices rise, a hymn of peace,
In spirit's arms, we find release.

Each soul shines with its own glow,
Together in the ebb and flow,
Bound by faith, through trials we tread,
In unity, our spirits led.

We gather close, the circle wide,
With whispered prayers, we do abide,
In every heartbeat, love resides,
Through every storm, our light confides.

So let us walk this holy path,
In kindness sown, we reap love's math,
For in this life, we intertwine,
United in spirit, truly divine.

A Symphony of Souls Aligned

In harmony, our voices blend,
A sacred bond, where hearts transcend,
Each note a prayer, a vibrant sound,
In this embrace, true peace is found.

With every breath, we lift our praise,
To the One who lights our ways,
Together singing in the night,
Our spirits soar, in shared delight.

The melody of love does call,
In unity, we rise and fall,
A symphony of life and grace,
Each soul a note in sacred space.

We walk as one, through joy and strife,
In the dance of ever-changing life,
With open hearts, we find our place,
In the music, we feel His embrace.

So let us play this grand design,
Our souls align, forever shine,
In this concert, we find our home,
Together, nevermore alone.

Whispers of Unity in Silence

In quiet moments, hearts conjoin,
Beneath the hush, the light we join,
In stillness found, our spirits meet,
A gentle pulse, our souls repeat.

The sacred breath, a sigh of grace,
Within the silence, we find our space,
A whispered word, a shared embrace,
In unity, our fears we face.

Time stands still as peace unfolds,
In every heart, a story told,
Through silent prayers, we rise anew,
In love's sweet bond, our spirits grew.

Each heartbeat echoes, soft and true,
In moments shared, we heal the blue,
Together, we create the light,
In whispered unity, we take flight.

So let us cherish this sacred pause,
In every silence, find the cause,
For in the stillness, He is near,
In whispered love, we have no fear.

The Divine Tapestry of Love

With threads of hope, our lives interlace,
In the loom of faith, we find our place,
Each story woven in His design,
A tapestry of love divine.

Colors vibrant, rich and bright,
In every hue, a guiding light,
We share our joys, our deepest sorrows,
In faith, we rise to meet tomorrow.

The fabric strong, yet soft we weave,
In love's embrace, we choose to believe,
Together bound by grace so sweet,
In every thread, His love we greet.

Through trials faced, our spirits soar,
In unity, we seek and explore,
For in this world, we are entwined,
A sacred bond, in love defined.

So let our hearts weave day by day,
In this divine dance, we find our way,
The tapestry of life we share,
In love's embrace, forever rare.

Embers of Faith

In the quiet night, hope glows bright,
A spark within, dispelling fright.
Hearts unite, forging a ray,
In strength we rise, come what may.

Whispers of grace in shadows cast,
Guiding light from the past.
A tapestry woven with love's embrace,
Together we find our sacred place.

Each prayer we lift, a song divine,
Trust in the path where spirits align.
Through trials faced, we stand as one,
In the heat of struggle, our faith is spun.

Faith like embers, warm and true,
Rekindled in the hearts of few.
A flame of hope burning ever bright,
Illuminating the path of light.

Kindled as One

In the circle drawn, hands entwine,
Souls united, a sacred sign.
Kindled with purpose, shining bold,
Together we share the stories told.

Each voice a note in harmony,
Singing praise, setting us free.
With every prayer, our spirits soar,
A bond unbroken forevermore.

Through valleys low and mountains high,
Side by side, we reach for the sky.
In trials faced, our spirits ignite,
Kindled as one, we walk in light.

Love like a river, flowing near,
Together we rise, casting out fear.
In unity's grace, our hearts entwined,
A tapestry of faith combined.

In the Embrace of Sacred Serenity

In stillness found, our spirits rest,
Wrapped in peace, we are truly blessed.
In the embrace of love divine,
Together we seek the sacred sign.

Across the meadows, whispers call,
In silence deep, we hear it all.
A gentle breeze, the spirit's song,
Reminding us where we all belong.

Each moment shared, a treasure rare,
In sacred bonds, we lay our care.
In the warmth of faith, we gently sway,
Walking the path in a holy way.

Here in this space, serenity glows,
Guiding us softly where the river flows.
Heartbeats echo, a sacred tune,
In love's embrace, we find our boon.

The Luminous Path of Togetherness

Together we tread, hand in hand,
On the luminous path, we take our stand.
Each step a blessing, a chance to grow,
In light's embrace, love will flow.

Memories crafted, like stars in the night,
Guiding our way, through darkness to light.
With every heartbeat, a sacred dance,
A journey shared, a divine chance.

In laughter and sorrow, we find our bond,
Every moment cherished, of which we're fond.
Through seasons changing, our love remains,
The luminous path that forever sustains.

In unity's grace, our spirits rise,
Illuminated hearts, touching the skies.
Together we walk, our souls aligned,
On this path of light, forever entwined.

The Vessel of Shared Blessings

In the vessel of love, blessings flow,
   Intertwined fates in harmony grow.
   Each act of kindness, a spark anew,
  Together we shine, in all we do.

From hearts filled with grace, we gather round,
   Sharing our joys that truly abound.
  In laughter shared, our spirits take flight,
 A symphony sung in the still of the night.

  With open hands, we give and receive,
  In the circle of faith, we duly believe.
  Each moment of giving brings us near,
  The vessel of blessings, crystal clear.

  In gratitude's glow, we lift our praise,
For the gift of connection, in all of our days.
  Together we flourish, evolving as one,
The vessel of shared blessings, forever begun.

Flowing Together in Love's River

In love's river, we find our way,
Hearts united, come what may.
Each ripple tells a tale divine,
In sacred flow, your heart meets mine.

With every wave, our spirits soar,
Together, we are evermore.
The current strong, yet gentle kiss,
In love's river, we find bliss.

As seasons change, our course may shift,
Yet love remains a timeless gift.
We trust the depths, we trust the tides,
In harmony, our souls abide.

The sun will rise, the moon will gleam,
In flowing waters, we will dream.
With faith as oars, we navigate,
In love's river, we celebrate.

Forever bound, our hearts will gleam,
Cast upon this sacred stream.
Together bound, in joy we strive,
Flowing gently, we are alive.

The Dance of Interwoven Spirits

In twilight's glow, our spirits meet,
In holy dance, we feel the beat.
Each step we take, a whisper shared,
With grace divine, we're unprepared.

Around us twirls the cosmic fife,
In harmony, we weave our life.
Entwined in faith, our souls align,
Together in this sacred sign.

Through trials faced, in joy we bind,
In every step, love's threads we find.
The rhythm calls, we lift our voice,
In unity, we make our choice.

With every twirl, we shed the past,
In love's embrace, our bonds hold fast.
As starlight guides this sacred chase,
In divinity, we find our place.

Our hearts alight, in reverence true,
This dance we share, both me and you.
With open arms, we seek the light,
In timeless grace, we take our flight.

In the Embrace of a Shared Journey

As path unfolds beneath our feet,
Together, every joy we meet.
In quiet strength, our spirits seek,
With love, the words we fail to speak.

Side by side, we face the dawn,
In sacred trust, we journey on.
Through mountains high and valleys deep,
In shared embrace, our hearts will leap.

The stars above guide our way,
In every moment, let us pray.
In trials faced, we stand as one,
In darkest nights, we find the sun.

With gentle hands and open hearts,
We forge a bond that never parts.
In laughter shared and tears released,
In sacred love, we find our peace.

So let us walk this path of light,
In joy and sorrow, day and night.
In every step, we find our song,
Together, where we both belong.

Where Harmony Meets Divine Grace

In whispers soft, we hear the call,
Where harmony shall bridge the wall.
In every note, a prayer ascends,
In sacred space, our spirit blends.

Beneath the stars, our hearts will sing,
In quiet grace, we feel the wing.
With every chord, we find our way,
In unity, we shape the day.

Through trials faced with faith so bold,
In grace divine, our story's told.
Each moment shared, a gift we give,
In love's embrace, we choose to live.

Together weaving threads of light,
In every word, a spirit bright.
With open hearts, let us embrace,
Where harmony meets divine grace.

So take my hand, let us unite,
In melodies that feel so right.
In every song, our souls will rise,
In perfect peace, where love never dies.

The Harmonious Spirit

In whispers soft, the Spirit sings,
Uniting hearts with fragile wings.
In grace we find our common ground,
In love's embrace, we're truly found.

Through trials faced, together stood,
In faith and hope, we find the good.
With every prayer, our souls align,
The harmonious oath, forever divine.

With every smile, the light we share,
A sacred bond beyond compare.
In unity, our strength is born,
A tapestry of hearts, reborn.

In quiet moments, truth revealed,
In kindness given, wounds are healed.
Through laughter shared, in joy we thrive,
In this spirit, we come alive.

With open hearts, we seek the grace,
In humble acts, our love we trace.
Each soul a note in life's grand song,
A harmonious spirit, where we belong.

In the Garden of Togetherness

In gardens lush, where blossoms grow,
Together we tend, through joy and woe.
With hands entwined, our roots run deep,
In sacred trust, our promises keep.

The sun that shines on all we share,
Illuminates our love and care.
With each soft breeze, our spirits rise,
In this rare place, our hearts align.

Time weaves its path, but we remain,
In every tear, in every gain.
In laughter's glow, in sorrow's shade,
In every moment, love displayed.

With gentle hearts, we sow the seeds,
In giving freely, fulfilling needs.
Together we'll weather any storm,
In this garden, our souls are warm.

Through every season, side by side,
In our embrace, we'll ever bide.
In the garden, where love is blessed,
Togetherness finds its purest rest.

Threads of Preparedness

In woven threads, our spirits meet,
With every stitch, our lives are sweet.
In preparation, we plant the seeds,
In faith's embrace, we find our needs.

With open hearts, we seek the light,
In every challenge, wrong or right.
Through trials faced, we stand upright,
With love as shield, we face the night.

In moments frail, we gather near,
In whispered prayers, we conquer fear.
With every thread, a purpose spun,
In unity, we are as one.

With open hands, we share the load,
Together we walk this sacred road.
In every heart, a promise kept,
Through love's embrace, our souls have leapt.

As dawn awakens, so do we,
In threads of hope, we're bound to be.
In shining light, our path is clear,
Prepared for grace, our hearts sincere.

Boundless Love

In boundless love, our spirits soar,
A gift that thrives, forevermore.
In every glance, a sacred vow,
In tender grace, we live the now.

With every heartbeat, bonds are forged,
In silent prayers, our souls are gorged.
Through winds of change, we stand as one,
In shadows cast, our light is spun.

In acts of kindness, small and grand,
Together we rise, hand in hand.
With every word, a passion flows,
In boundless depths, our garden grows.

In stormy seas and calm, we trust,
In love's embrace, our hearts combust.
Through time unending, we endure,
In boundless love, our souls are pure.

With every breath, we live the grace,
In shared laughter, we find our place.
In unity's glow, forever drawn,
Boundless love, our joyful dawn.

Transcending Time

In timeless grace, our souls entwine,
Beyond the stars, a love divine.
In every moment, sacred sighs,
Transcending time, our spirits rise.

With whispered dreams, we navigate,
In love's embrace, we celebrate.
In fleeting hours, a promise made,
Transcending time, we will not fade.

In every heartbeat, echoes strong,
In harmony, where we belong.
Through ages past, our essence flows,
Transcending time, forever glows.

With every kiss, a universe,
In woven paths, our hearts immerse.
Through history's dance, our story's told,
Transcending time, in love's pure gold.

As daylight fades and night draws near,
In every breath, you will be here.
Through whispers soft, in twilight's chime,
Transcending all, our hearts combine.

Tender Threads of Devotion

In whispers soft, the prayers arise,
Each heart a candle, glowing bright.
Transcending time, under vast skies,
We weave our faith, a sacred light.

With every breath, we seek His grace,
Hands uplifted, we humbly bow.
In trials faced, we find His face,
With love's embrace, we heed the vow.

Through laughter shared and tears that fall,
We find in silence, His gentle call.
With tender threads, our souls entwine,
Devotion's bond, pure and divine.

In sacred space, our spirits soar,
Journeying close, forevermore.
Each moment cherished, every prayer,
In faith's embrace, we find our share.

Time bends gently to love's pure song,
In tender hearts, we all belong.
Through storms and peace, our spirits blend,
In life's mosaic, we ascend.

The Altar of Our Spirits

At dawn's first light, we gather near,
The altar set, our souls align.
With hopes and dreams, we cast our fear,
In stillness found, the heart's design.

Each prayer a rose, fragrant and rare,
In gratitude, we lift our voice.
Through trials faced, in love we share,
Together strong, we make our choice.

As seasons change, our faith remains,
In every loss, a lesson learned.
Through joy and sorrow, love sustains,
In spirit's warmth, all hearts are turned.

By candle's glow, our wishes burn,
In whispered hopes, the sacred yearn.
With every stone, a story told,
The altar stands, both brave and bold.

United here, our spirits rise,
In sacred bonds, we find our prize.
From heart to heart, the light we share,
The altar holds our faith and care.

Mandala of the Soul's Journey

In circles drawn, our lives unfold,
A mandala rich with colors bright.
Each line a tale, like threads of gold,
In the heart's canvas, find the light.

With every step, a truth revealed,
In sacred dance, our spirits flow.
Through sacred paths, our fate is sealed,
The soul's journey, ever aglow.

Moments shared, in laughter's sound,
In unity, our voices blend.
With each return, new wisdom found,
In love's embrace, our hearts attend.

Through storm and calm, the circle binds,
In every hue, the spirit sings.
A mandala formed by loving minds,
In joy and grace, our freedom brings.

Together strong, we paint the sky,
In every journey, we learn to fly.
In this grand design, we find our way,
A tapestry woven, night and day.

In Exalted Union

In sacred space, our hearts collide,
In exalted union, love ignites.
With every breath, we cast aside,
The veils that dim our shared delights.

Through spirit's voice, we feel the call,
In stillness found, our souls embrace.
No longer alone, we rise and fall,
Together bound, we seek His grace.

With hands entwined, we walk this path,
Each step a dance of hope anew.
In love's sweet glow, we face the wrath,
From trials faced, our faith shines through.

In worship pure, we sing as one,
United hearts beneath the sun.
With open arms, we find our home,
In exalted union, we shall roam.

As dawn breaks forth, our spirits dance,
In love's embrace, we take our chance.
Together now, forever free,
In sacred union, you and me.

Radiance of Together

In unity we stand, hand in hand,
Glowing with a light so grand.
Each heart a beacon, shining bright,
Together we rise, embracing the light.

With faith as our bond, we shall thrive,
In the warmth of love, we come alive.
Every prayer, a whispered plea,
In this sacred space, we are free.

Through trials and storms, we hold tight,
Guided by grace, we find our sight.
In the depth of night, we see the dawn,
A promise of hope, forever drawn.

Together we sing, voices entwined,
In the chorus of souls, divinely aligned.
With every note, our spirits soar,
In the radiance of together, we explore.

As we journey forth, fear cast aside,
In the light of love, forever we bide.
For in this union, we find our way,
In the radiance of together, we stay.

Cherished in the Embrace of Belief

In the warmth of grace, we find our peace,
Cherished in love, our worries cease.
Hand in hand, we tread life's road,
In the embrace of belief, we lighten the load.

Each step a prayer, our hearts align,
In the sanctuary of faith, our spirits shine.
With whispers of hope, we climb and ascend,
Together we find, on each other we depend.

Through trials we face, we gather strength,
In the tapestry of love, we find our length.
With every heartbeat, a promise bestowed,
Cherished and held, in our sacred abode.

Our voices in chorus, a hymn of love,
Guided by light from the heavens above.
In every tear, in every smile,
Cherished in the embrace, we journey each mile.

As seasons change and time flows,
In the garden of faith, our spirit grows.
United in trust, we rise and breathe,
Cherished in the embrace, forever we weave.

The Sacred Circle

In the sacred circle, where souls unite,
Bound by compassion, shining bright.
With hearts open wide, we share our grace,
In this haven of love, we find our place.

Each voice a thread, woven in time,
In the dance of faith, we create our rhyme.
Gathered together, we share our light,
In the sacred circle, we embrace the night.

With hands held high, we raise our song,
In the warmth of forgiveness, we all belong.
Every story told, a treasure to keep,
In the sacred circle, our spirits leap.

Through trials faced and mountains climbed,
In this circle of love, we are aligned.
As stars above, we twinkle and shine,
In the sacred circle, our souls entwine.

Together we stand, fearless and free,
In the circle of hope, we find our decree.
Each heart a flame, warming the cold,
In the sacred circle, our stories unfold.

Communion of Kindred Hearts

In the communion of hearts, we resonate,
Tuned to the melody of love innate.
With every word, we build a bridge,
Connecting our spirits, a sacred edge.

Through laughter and tears, we share the night,
In the warmth of kinship, we find our light.
Together we wander, hand in hand,
In the communion of kindred, we understand.

With each heartbeat, a rhythm divine,
In this sacred dance, our souls entwine.
Every prayer shared, a light in the dark,
In the communion of kindred, we leave a mark.

As shadows may fall, and storms arise,
In the strength of each other, we find the wise.
With courage as armor and faith as our shield,
In the communion of hearts, we are healed.

Through trials we rise, with spirits aflame,
In the embrace of the kindred, we speak the same name.
Together we grow, forever impart,
In the communion of kindred hearts.

Beacons of Holiness

In silence, we gather, hearts aglow,
Guided by light that eternally shows.
Hands lifted high, seeking His grace,
In moments of stillness, we find our place.

Belief in His love, a flame that ignites,
Shining through darkness, illuminating nights.
With every prayer, a bond is reborn,
In sacred whispers, our spirits are sworn.

Each soul a vessel, each heart a song,
Together we rise, united and strong.
The echoes of faith in our gentle breath,
In the dance of devotion, we conquer death.

Hope is our anchor, trust is our chain,
Through valleys of sorrow, we rise again.
In trials, we stand, with courage to fight,
For in love's embrace, we find the light.

The path illuminated by prayers sincere,
Each step a testament, drawing us near.
In the beacons of holiness, we find our way,
Guided by love, come what may.

Bonds Forged in Faith

In the quiet moments, hearts align,
Whispers of love, a sacred sign.
Together we walk, hand in hand,
In the garden of grace, we take our stand.

Through trials faced, our spirits grow,
In the warmth of faith, our souls will glow.
Each prayer a thread, forming the weave,
A tapestry rich in what we believe.

We rise as one, through storm and strife,
Bonded in faith, the essence of life.
In shadows cast, His light will shine,
Creating a bond, eternally divine.

The beauty of patience, the power of grace,
In the hands of the faithful, a sacred space.
With every heartbeat, love's rhythm flows,
In bonds forged in faith, our spirit grows.

United we soar, like eagles in flight,
Even in darkness, we carry the light.
Together in spirit, forever we stand,
Believing in truth, shared hearts, and hands.

Echoes of Heavenly Connection

In the stillness of dawn, voices arise,
Whispers of angels, beneath endless skies.
Every prayer uttered, a resonance strong,
In echoes of faith, we are never wrong.

A chorus of hearts, united in song,
In the church of the spirit, where we all belong.
Moments of silence, a sacred embrace,
Through the echoes of love, we find His grace.

In trials together, we sing our plight,
Through valleys of shadow, we seek the light.
Connected by faith, with each sacred breath,
In the echoes of Heaven, we conquer death.

The joy of belonging, each soul intertwined,
In the garden of prayer, our spirits aligned.
With hearts open wide, we dance in delight,
For the echoes of love carry us through night.

In bonds of devotion, our voices unite,
Through whispers of mercy, we shine ever bright.
In the echoing silence, we bravely tread,
Relying on love, for love is our thread.

The Sacred Fusion

In the womb of creation, love took its form,
From chaos emerged, a promise to warm.
In hearts that are open, divine light shines,
In the sacred fusion, our spirit aligns.

Moments of splendor, through suffering shared,
In the tapestry woven, we find how we're bared.
The power of unity, a force that instills,
Through the sacred fusion, love endlessly fills.

With every step forward, hand in hand,
The vision of harmony, brightly we stand.
In trials and triumphs, we rise and we soar,
Fueled by the promise of love evermore.

Through silence and prayer, connection grows deep,
In the sacred fusion, our vigil we keep.
Every tear shed, a testament made,
To the bonds we embrace in love's sweet cascade.

In the heart of the faithful, we gather as one,
Embracing the journey, until it is done.
For in every moment, forever we cling,
In the sacred fusion, our praises we sing.

United Under the Skies of Belief

Beneath the stars, we gather as one,
Hearts entwined, our journey begun.
Faith our anchor, through storms we sail,
In unity strong, we shall prevail.

Together we rise, with spirits ablaze,
Worshiping love in myriad ways.
Hands held high, our voices shared,
In sacred bonds, we are prepared.

With every prayer, our souls take flight,
Chasing the shadows with radiant light.
In harmony's dance, we find our place,
Embodied grace, our hearts embrace.

Through trials faced, we find our strength,
In every step, we go the length.
Guided by stars, our visions clear,
In unity's warmth, we cast out fear.

So let us soar, 'neath heavens above,
United in purpose, boundless in love.
With faith as our guide, hand in hand we roam,
Together forever, we are home.

The Flame of Fellowship

In the flicker's glow, our spirits align,
From each spark arise, a love divine.
Together we breathe in the warmth of grace,
Sharing the light, in this holy space.

With every whisper, a promise we make,
In the heart's chorus, no soul shall break.
Gathered as one, we kindle the fire,
Fellowship strong, our souls inspired.

Each flame unique, yet joined as one,
Illustrates the love that cannot be shunned.
With laughter and tears, through joy and strife,
We celebrate the essence of life.

As shadows fade, and night drifts away,
The embers of friendship eternally stay.
For in each heartbeat, we find our way,
Together we shine, come what may.

So let us hold this flame so bright,
Nurture the bond in day and night.
In the warmth of our unity, we stand tall,
Bound by the flame that unites us all.

Ever Bright

In the dawn's embrace, we rise anew,
Under skies of hope, we seek what's true.
With hearts aglow, our spirits soar,
In the light of love, forevermore.

Each dawn a promise, each dusk a grace,
In the cycle of time, we find our place.
Guided by faith, we chase the light,
Together as one, our path is bright.

From whispered prayers to joyous songs,
In every heartbeat, together we belong.
Embracing change, our journey's a flight,
With inner peace, we shine our light.

Through trials faced, we grow much stronger,
In love's embrace, we fear no longer.
With open hearts, our vision wide,
Ever bright, we walk side by side.

So let our spirits raise high the flame,
In love's sweet whisper, we're never the same.
For in unity's arms, we find our bliss,
Ever bright is this sacred kiss.

Connected in Spirit's Embrace

In the quiet moments, we find our peace,
Connected in spirit, our joys increase.
With every thought, a bond we weave,
In the core of love, we dare believe.

The whispers of souls, a melodious song,
In harmony's embrace, we all belong.
Through trials we face, hand in hand we stand,
United and strong, heart to heart, we land.

In the dance of life, we twirl and sway,
Embracing the journey, come what may.
With laughter resounding, like rain from above,
In every heartbeat, we find our love.

As the sun sets low, and the moon starts to rise,
In this sacred place, we gaze at the skies.
With gratitude deep, for all we've embraced,
Connected in spirit, our fears we've faced.

So let our hearts shine with hope and grace,
In love's gentle warmth, we find our place.
For in every moment, together we thrive,
Connected in spirit, forever alive.

The Universe of Love in Unity

In the vast expanse, where stardust twirls,
Awakening hearts in a world that swirls.
One love unites, in every embrace,
A universe formed in divine grace.

From mountains high to oceans deep,
In nature's cradle, our dreams we keep.
Threaded in love, our spirits entwined,
In the cosmos vast, our purpose aligned.

With open arms, we welcome the light,
In every struggle, we find our might.
With courage and hope, we chart the course,
For love is the beacon, our only source.

As galaxies spin, through time and space,
The essence of love we boldly embrace.
In unity's rhythm, we dance and sing,
In one vibrant heart, we are everything.

With every heartbeat, the universe sways,
In love's gentle touch, we count the days.
For in unity's arms, we're whole and free,
A universe thriving, in harmony.

Anointing the Collective Soul

In silence we gather, one heart aligned,
A sacred breath blesses the space,
Together we rise, in love intertwined,
Anointing the world with our grace.

Each whisper of prayer touches the sky,
Hands lifted high, we beckon the light,
In unity's bond, we never say goodbye,
Embracing the warmth of divine might.

Through trials we wander, yet never alone,
In fellowship's comfort, we find our way,
The spirit resides in the seeds we have sown,
Eternal the love that we share every day.

With gratitude flowing like rivers so pure,
We walk as pilgrims on this holy ground,
To nurture the flame, forever secure,
Anointing each soul with a sacred sound.

The echoes of kindness, the songs that we sing,
Resound through the ages, they echo and swell,
In the dance of creation, our spirits take wing,
Anointing the world with a love we know well.

Interwoven Paths of Grace

In the tapestry woven by hands of the divine,
Threads of our journeys entwine with care,
A dance of existence, a sacred design,
With grace as our guide, we wander and share.

Each step that we take is a blessing bestowed,
In the light of compassion, we find our way,
As rivers converge on the journey we rode,
Interwoven in love, we embrace each day.

Through valleys of shadows and mountains so wide,
We rise with the dawn, side by side,
In the arms of the Spirit, our fears we confide,
Trusting in grace that forever will bide.

With hearts open wide, we gather and sing,
The symphony echoes, a beautiful sound,
In the embrace of each moment, the joy that we bring,
Interwoven paths where true love is found.

For in every heartbeat, in every soft prayer,
We find the connection that binds us as one,
A radiant promise that lingers in air,
Interwoven paths, where grace has begun.

The Celestial Covenant

In the heavens above, a promise unfolds,
A covenant written in starlight and dreams,
With whispers of angels, in stories retold,
The sacred connection flows in gentle streams.

Each soul is a vessel, a beacon of light,
Carrying wisdom from ages gone by,
With faith as our anchor, we shine ever bright,
In the celestial dance, our spirits will fly.

Through tears and through laughter, we tread this earth,
In the sacred embrace of creation we dwell,
For every lost moment has infinite worth,
In the fabric of time, we weave our own spell.

The echoes of love rise like incense in prayer,
A tapestry woven with threads soft and rare,
Each heart finds its rhythm, a song to declare,
That in the celestial, our spirits lay bare.

In the harmony spoken, our voices unite,
The celestial covenant, a promise of grace,
With hands joined together, we stand in the light,
For together in love, we shall find our true place.

Essence of the Many

From the whispers of ages, we come as a whole,
The essence of many, in truth we reside,
Each story and heartbeat a part of the soul,
In the garden of life, we flourish with pride.

With colors united, diversity shines,
In the cradle of spirit, our differences blend,
In laughter and struggle, a pathway defines,
The essence of many, together we mend.

As mountains and valleys embrace in their grace,
So we find our purpose, in service we grow,
In the light of compassion, every smile has a place,
The essence of many, in love we bestow.

We gather as one, a celestial choir,
With harmonies echoing across every land,
In the fire of kindness, our spirits aspire,
The essence of many, in unity stand.

In the stillness of night, our hearts intertwine,
Each prayer a reflection of light shining bright,
For in every connection, the stars align,
The essence of many, forever in flight.

Spirit of the One

In the hush of creation, the Spirit unfolds,
A whisper of love, transcending the night,
In the warmth of the heart, a flame brightly holds,
Guiding each soul towards the infinite light.

With eyes that can see, we gather in grace,
The Spirit of One, in moments so still,
Each heartbeat a rhythm, each breath we embrace,
In the bond of our oneness, our spirits fulfill.

Through valleys of doubt and mountains of hope,
We journey together, our voices are strong,
Each step a reflection, together we cope,
In the Spirit of One, we find where we belong.

As dawn greets the earth with her radiant glow,
We rise with the promise of love to appear,
In every connection, the truth will bestow,
The Spirit of One, ever present, so near.

With hearts intertwined, we walk hand in hand,
In the circle of life, no soul stands apart,
For the Spirit of One is a love ever grand,
In the fabric of being, we each play a part.

Where Souls Converge in Prayer

In silence deep, we gather near,
The whispers lift, a voice so clear.
Hands entwined, our spirits rise,
United hearts beneath the skies.

In sacred halls, where faith ignites,
We seek the truth, embrace the light.
Each humble plea, a fragrant prayer,
In love's embrace, we lay our care.

Through trials faced, our hearts will sing,
The bonds of grace, forever cling.
In fervent hope, our spirits soar,
Together strong, we ask for more.

With every breath, we share our needs,
In gentle faith, our spirit feeds.
The heavens hear our quiet search,
As souls converge in sacred church.

As light descends, our shadows fade,
With every prayer, new paths are laid.
Here in this space, we come alive,
Where souls converge, and love will thrive.

The Light of Many Flames

A candle lit with hope untold,
Reflects the warmth that we uphold.
In darkest nights, our flames will gleam,
Together, we ignite the dream.

Each spark a prayer, a wish profound,
In unity, our hearts abound.
With tender grace, our spirits blend,
The light of love that will not end.

From different paths, we gather close,
In harmony, our souls engross.
Through trials faced, we shine so bright,
In the light of many flames, pure light.

With every flicker, stories blend,
In whispered words, we will transcend.
A tapestry of dreams we weave,
In this embrace, we all believe.

As shadows wane, we lift our song,
Where many flames unite, we're strong.
Together here, let love reclaim,
The world transformed, in light of flame.

Eternal Kinship Under Heaven

Beneath the vast and starlit sky,
We find our kinship, you and I.
In every heart, a bond so true,
Eternal ties that pull us through.

From distant lands, in faith we stand,
With open hearts, in love unplanned.
Each solemn vow, a promise made,
Under heaven's watch, we are not frayed.

In laughter shared and sorrows grieved,
Our spirit's dance, we have believed.
With every tear, with every cheer,
Eternal kinship draws us near.

Through winding roads, our journey bold,
With stories shared, forever told.
In sacred circles, hand in hand,
We navigate this promised land.

When trials come, we stand as one,
In hope alive, till day is done.
For in this love, we are ascended,
Eternal kinship, souls defended.

Unfurling the Petals of the Heart

In tender dawn, the petals wake,
With morning light, we gently take.
Each burst of bloom, a love anew,
As hearts unfold, pure and true.

Through gentle hands, we nurture dreams,
In whispered hopes, our purpose beams.
With every petal, wisdom shared,
Our inner light, forever bared.

With every joy, a fragrance sweet,
In joy and pain, we find our seat.
In nature's grace, we come alive,
Unfurling hearts, where spirits thrive.

With open souls, we share our fears,
In sacred trust, we dry the tears.
The beauty found within the scars,
Unfurling hearts, we reach the stars.

As seasons change, we grow and bend,
In love's embrace, we find our mend.
In unity, our petals part,
Unfurling gently, the beating heart.

Milton Keynes UK
Ingram Content Group UK Ltd.
UKHW021913201124
451474UK00013B/725